STEM Careers

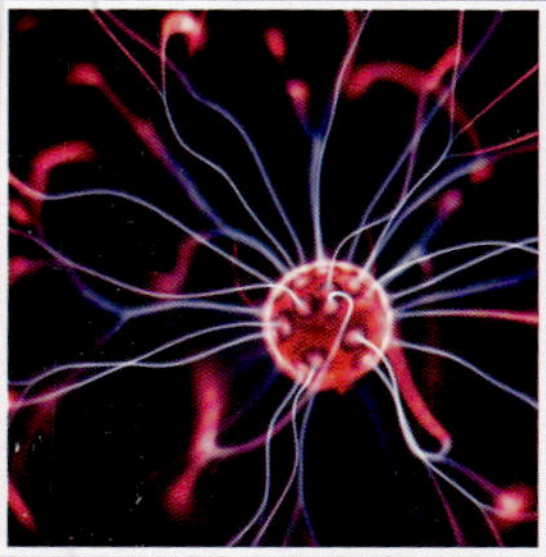

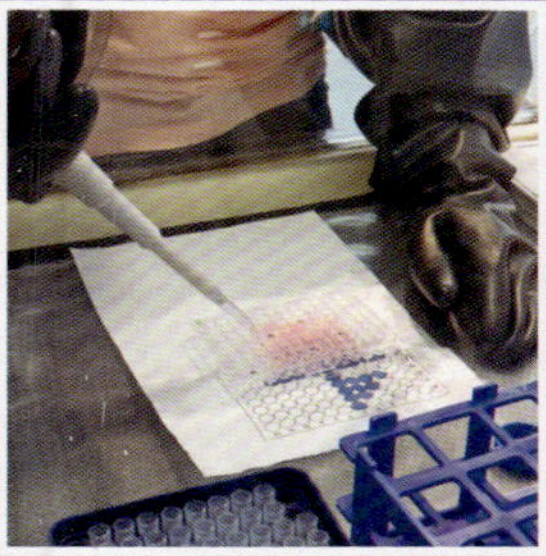

PHYSICIST

Tammy Gagne and
Heather Kissock

AV2
www.av2books.com

AV2

Step 1
Go to **www.av2books.com**

Step 2
Enter this unique code
QNCPR7IO5

Step 3
Explore your interactive eBook!

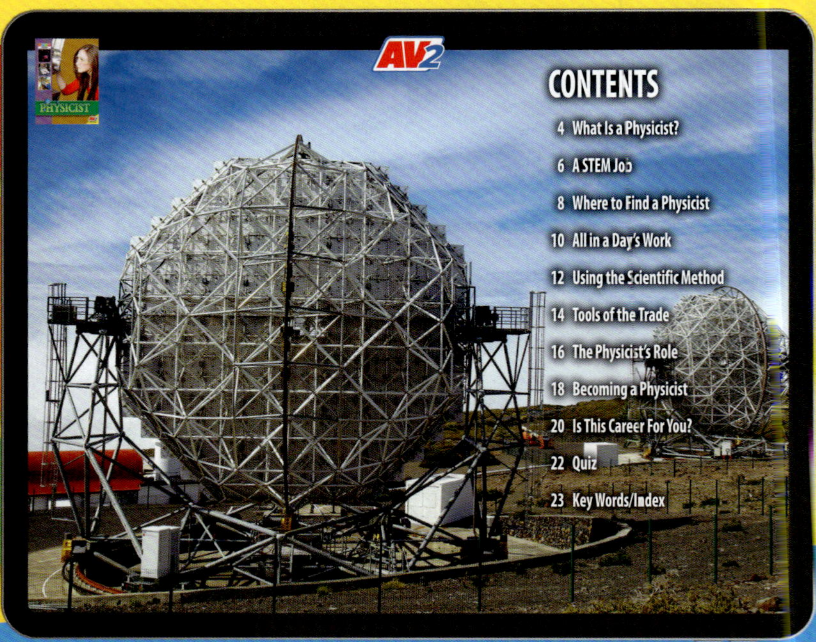

AV2 is optimized for use on any device

Your interactive eBook comes with...

Contents
Browse a live contents page to easily navigate through resources

Audio
Listen to sections of the book read aloud

Videos
Watch informative video clips

Weblinks
Gain additional information for research

Try This!
Complete activities and hands-on experiments

Key Words
Study vocabulary, and complete a matching word activity

Quizzes
Test your knowledge

Slideshows
View images and captions

... and much, much more!

STEM Careers

PHYSICIST

Contents

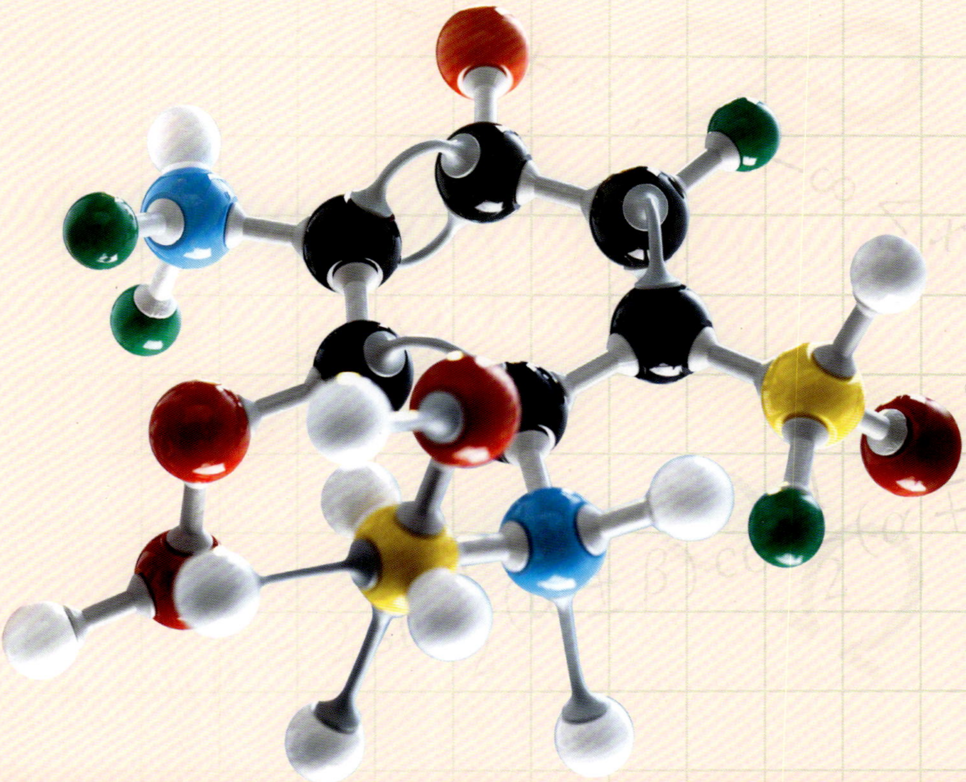

What Is a Physicist?

Physics is the science of **matter** and energy. Scientists who specialize in the study of physics are called physicists. A physicist may study any of a number of branches of physics. This list includes electricity, **mechanics**, and the structure of atoms. These tiny particles are the building blocks of all matter.

Most physicists are naturally curious about the world. They want to know how and why things work the way they do. Some people might wonder why studying physics is worthwhile. After all, the human eye cannot even see an atom without the help of special microscopes. Physicists, however, know that the work they do is important. It was the study of atoms that led to the invention of such valuable tools as modern computers and **satellite** technology. Even a smartphone would not exist without the work of physicists.

Approximately **16,730** physicists work in the United States.

About **21 percent** of university physics teachers in the United States **are female**.

The **median salary** of a physicist in the United States is **$122,850**.

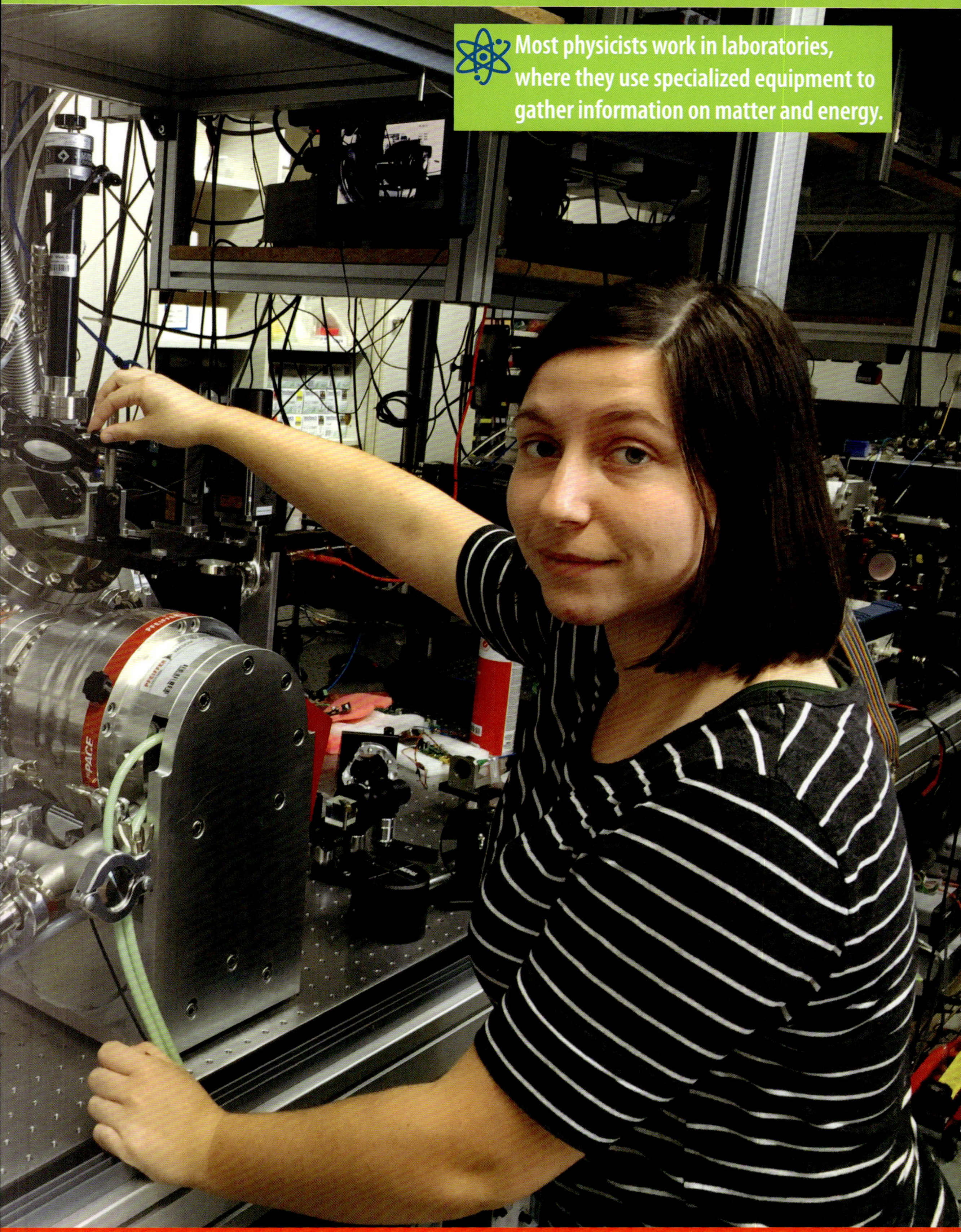

Most physicists work in laboratories, where they use specialized equipment to gather information on matter and energy.

A STEM Job

Physicists work in the field of STEM. STEM stands for Science, Technology, Engineering, and Mathematics, or math. STEM is a developing field. Jobs in STEM change as new tools and techniques are created.

Dealing with scientific concepts and **theories** forms the basis of a physicist's work. However, to do this, physicists must also have a good understanding of math. Which type of math a physicist uses depends on his or her field of work. Physicists who study nuclear physics use much more **calculus** than those who study molecular physics. This field uses more **algebra**.

Where Physicists Work

A person with a physics degree can work in a number of locations, depending on the focus of his or her work. California employs the most physicists. This is because there are many technology companies based in this state.

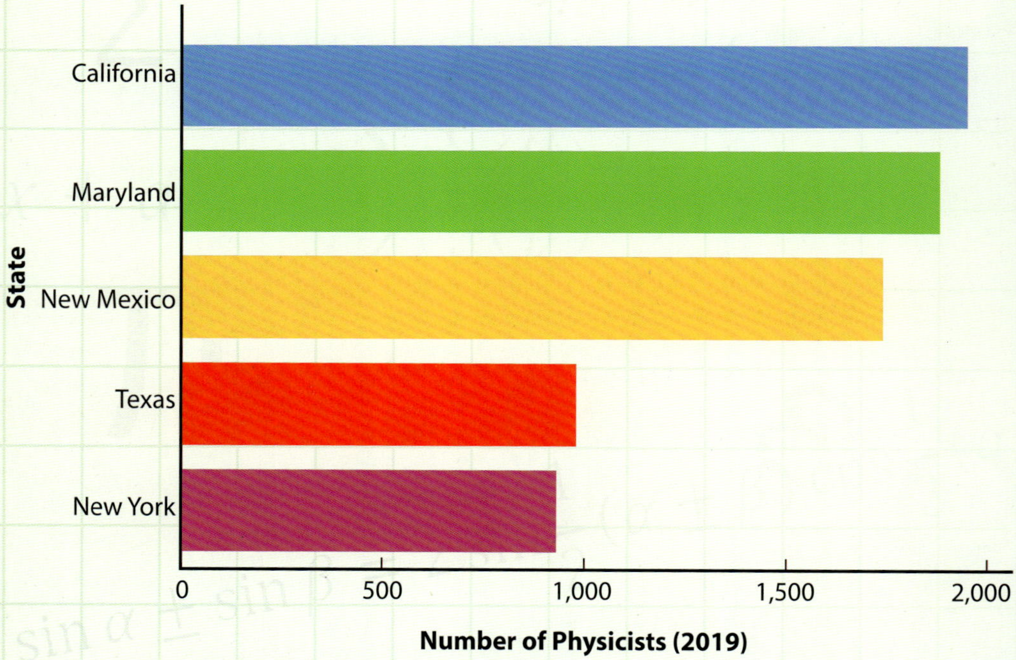

A physicist's work often connects to other STEM fields as well. Many physicists work alongside doctors, engineers, and even astronauts. Different types of physicists may also work on the same team for certain projects. Most STEM fields work to advance technology in one way or another.

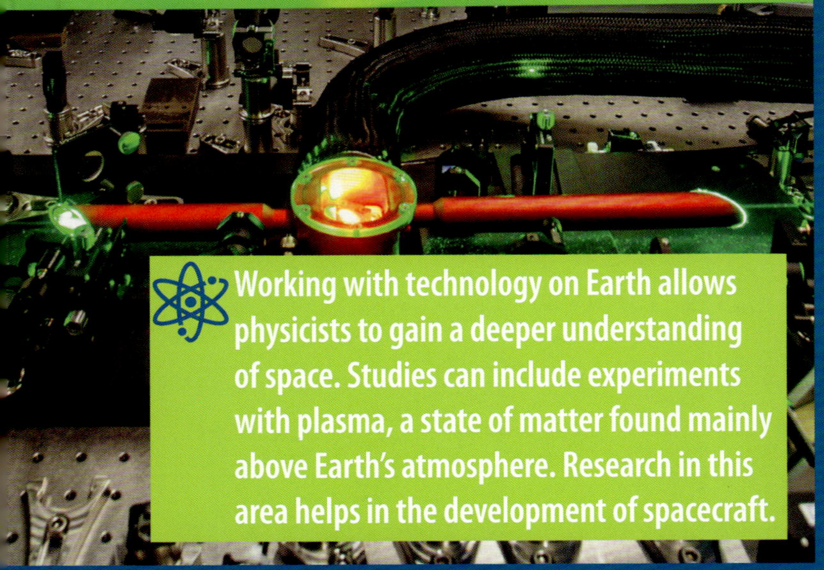

Working with technology on Earth allows physicists to gain a deeper understanding of space. Studies can include experiments with plasma, a state of matter found mainly above Earth's atmosphere. Research in this area helps in the development of spacecraft.

STEM

People working in STEM professions typically earn **26 percent** more than people working in non-STEM jobs.

Health care is one of the most popular STEM fields. Of the **9 million** Americans employed in this field, **75 percent** are women.

Only **52 percent** of people who train for STEM jobs are employed in them.

Where to Find a Physicist

A person with a physics degree can work in a variety of places. Many physicists find jobs in academic settings. They might work at universities or research facilities. Here, physicists spend much of their time working to confirm theories and trying to make new discoveries. Some physicists put their skills to use for technology companies. These include companies that manufacture telecommunications devices, such as tablets and cell phones.

Technology Employment in the United States

There are many types of technology employers in the United States. Physicists may specialize in telecommunications, space travel, air transportation, or health care equipment.

Boeing
Seattle, Washington

Apple Computers
Cupertino, California

Other physicists can be found working for hospitals and other health care organizations. Their jobs may involve developing new technologies or testing medical equipment. Energy companies also employ a high number of physicists. Some focus on extracting **fossil fuels** from the ground as efficiently as possible. Others work with **renewable resources**, such as water or wind. Unlike fossil fuels, these energy sources will never run out.

Microsoft
Redmond, Washington

NASA
Washington, D.C.

Physicists may be invited to speak about their work at science conferences and public lectures.

All in a Day's Work

An average day at work for a physicist depends greatly on the branch of physics he or she studies. Most physicists have to perform many of the same everyday tasks involved in other jobs, however. For example, many physicists have to return phone calls, answer emails, and attend meetings.

Other parts of being a physicist are more unique. For instance, an astrophysicist is someone who studies objects and events in space. Many of these physicists work with satellites. These machines collect data for physicists and other scientists to analyze. A satellite may send text messages to a physicist when it detects certain phenomena. Recording data from the satellite involves making many advanced mathematics calculations. Physicists draw important conclusions from this data. This, in turn, helps many other types of scientists learn more about space.

Sample Daily Schedule

An astrophysicist's day can include a number of tasks. It can also involve a fair amount of waiting for events to happen. While they wait, these physicists study the data they have already collected and share their knowledge with the rest of the world.

8:00 AM

An astrophysicist arrives at the university where she works. She heads into a meeting with the other physicists in her department. She has been writing a paper about **gamma ray** bursts for an academic journal. Working as a team, her coworkers offer input about her rough draft.

9:00 AM

Returning to her office, the astrophysicist resumes work on a computer **simulation** she is designing. She will use it to model the data from the last gamma ray burst she studied. The simulation will help others understand the information better.

11:00 AM

The astrophysicist participates in a conference call that includes astrophysicists from other parts of the world. They each share data from the projects they are working on.

12:00 PM

The astrophysicist takes her lunch break. She keeps her phone with her as she is expecting a text message from a satellite. The information it sends will help her with a study she is doing.

1:00 PM

Back in her office, the astrophysicist continues to work on her simulation. She must finish it before an upcoming meeting with engineers at the university. She also plans to use part of it as a visual aid during a speech she has been asked to deliver soon.

3:00 PM

The astrophysicist saves her work on the simulation and prepares to head across the campus. She teaches a class at the university for physics students pursuing their **master's degrees**.

Using the Scientific Method

Scientists use the scientific method to solve problems. The scientific method is a series of steps. It begins with a question scientists want to answer. First, the scientists find out if someone else has asked the same question. If so, they review that scientist's results and gather information for their work. Next, they make a hypothesis. This is what they think the answer to their question will be. The scientists then test the hypothesis with an experiment. After the experiment, they form a conclusion. This means they study the results and decide if the question was answered. Finally, the scientists share their results with the public and other scientists.

1. Ask a Question

Does an object's **density** affect the speed at which it will fall to the ground?

2. Construct a Hypothesis

In 1589, an Italian scientist named Galileo Galilei is said to have dropped two round objects from the top of a tower. The objects were the same size, but one was denser than the other. The two objects reached the ground at the same time. This information supports the hypothesis that a baseball and a tennis ball will also hit the ground simultaneously, even though the baseball has a higher density.

3. Test with an Experiment

To conduct this experiment, set up a step stool outdoors on level ground. While standing on the stool, drop a baseball and a tennis ball from the same height. Ask a friend to record the experiment on his or her phone. Perform it three times to make sure the results are consistent. Carefully review the videos for the results.

4. Did the Test Work?

The videos showed that both balls hit the ground at roughly the same moment each time they were dropped together.

5. Draw Conclusions

As both the baseball and tennis ball hit the ground at the same time, the experiment showed that density does not change the time it takes an object to fall to the ground.

Tools of the Trade

Physicists observe and measure objects that vary in size. To help with these processes, physicists use a variety of tools and instruments. Some help to magnify microscopic atoms. Others work to calculate the dimensions of astronomical objects.

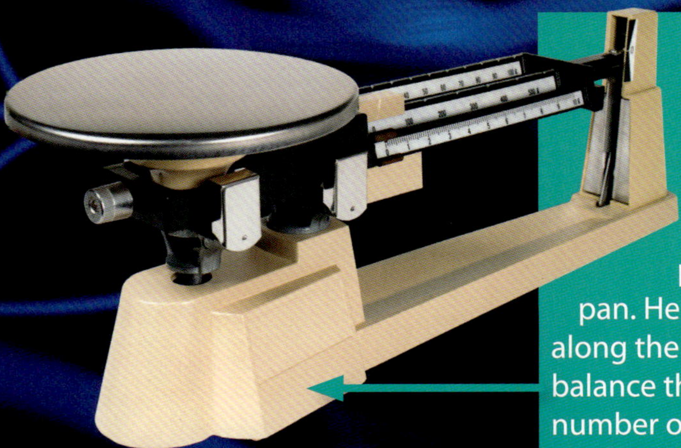

Beam Scale

A beam scale is a measuring device for determining an object's mass, or the quantity of matter it contains. To use this device, a physicist sets an object on the scale's pan. He or she then begins to slide weights along the scale's beams. When the beams balance the scale's pointer to zero, the location number of each weight is added together. The total is the mass of the object.

Laser

A laser is a device that generates a powerful beam of light. Lasers help physicists trap atoms in **vacuum chambers**. Atoms are always moving. By trapping them in these chambers, physicists can cool them and slow them down. This makes it easier for physicists to observe the atoms.

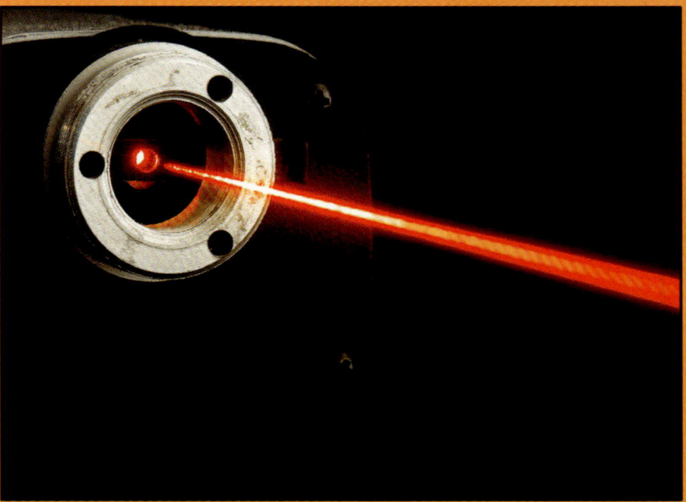

Plotting Compass

Physicists use plotting compasses to measure **magnetic fields**. These simple compasses are placed at different points around a magnet. By marking the direction that the needle points at each location, physicists can learn more about how magnetic fields function. They use this information to determine how magnetic forces work on Earth and in space.

Particle Accelerator

A particle accelerator breaks atoms up into smaller pieces. It then propels these pieces through a pipe. As the pieces move through the pipe, their energy level increases. Once they have reached a certain level, an object is put inside the pipe. Special instruments within the accelerator take readings of what happens when the particles collide with the object. Physicists use particle accelerators to learn more about how Earth and the universe came to be.

Balance Scales

Technology is constantly developing. New or updated equipment allows physicists to improve upon studies completed long ago. Questions that could not be answered can be revisited and explored in more detail. In some cases, however, traditional tools, such as balance scales, still have a place in scientific study.

Then

Created in ancient Egypt, balance scales were the first devices made to precisely measure mass. Most physics labs still have traditional balance scales on hand. They are mainly used to weigh large items.

Now

Today, physicists typically use digital scales for determining the mass of miniscule objects. Digital devices can measure an item's mass with an accuracy of 0.1 to 0.01 grams.

The Physicist's Role

The work of modern physicists covers a wide range of areas. This is due mainly to the discoveries of their predecessors. For example, x-rays were first discovered at the end of the 19th century. This form of **electromagnetic radiation** makes it possible to see people's bones from outside their bodies. Over the next century, physicists worked with x-rays to find ways that they could be used. X-ray machines soon led scientists to create CT scanners, which provided new types of views into the human body.

The MAGIC telescopes in Spain have provided physicists with data about black holes, supernovas, and other phenomena in deep space.

While these machines advanced medicine, they also expanded the work of modern physicists. Today, astrophysicists use x-ray telescopes to detect radiation coming from objects in deep space. This technology makes it possible for physicists to learn more about **black holes**, **supernovas**, and the possible origins of the universe. The study of x-rays also led to the discovery of DNA's structure. DNA is the molecule that carries a person's **genetic** information. Modern physicists can now explore deep inside the human body or deep into the universe, all because of the physicists who came before them.

Learning More about X-Rays

X-rays can show the insides of many different materials. Doctors and dentists use x-rays to look for cracks in a patient's bones or teeth. Airport security uses x-rays to look for dangerous items inside passengers' luggage. X-rays can even be used to find flaws in large structures such as buildings or bridges.

German scientist Wilhelm Röntgen discovered **x-rays** in **1895**.

Patients in the United States receive more than **80 million** medical x-rays each year.

An x-ray delivers about **10 million** times more energy than a radio wave.

Becoming a Physicist

People usually choose careers based on the tasks they excel at and most enjoy doing. Future physicists want to learn about the inner workings of their environment from a young age. As children, they are often seen taking their toys apart to see what is inside and how the pieces work together. Once in school, future physicists demonstrate a strong aptitude for the sciences. They excel at math and are often placed in advanced classes.

One of the best ways to explore a career as a physicist before choosing it as a path is by taking part in a physics camp. These camps provide hands-on opportunities for students to learn about light, sound, electricity, space, and numerous other physics topics. Many schools offer physics clubs for students who think they might want to pursue a degree in this subject after graduating from high school.

Physicist Salaries

A physicist's salary depends on his or her education, level of experience, and place of employment. Some physicists can make more than $175,000 per year.

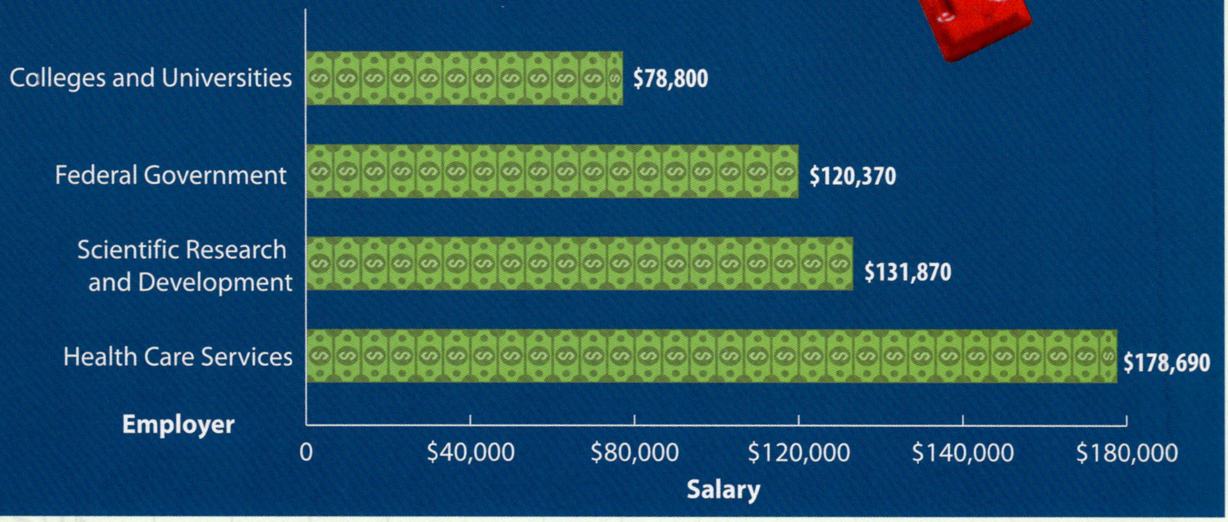

Potential physicists are drawn to events such as the First Robotics Competition, which sees students take robots they have built through several challenges.

Is This Career For You?

A physicist's job consists of doing extensive research. Anyone contemplating a career in this field should enjoy studying and learning about science. Potential physicists must also be willing to take advanced schooling. This can take years to complete.

Training

Training to become a physicist begins in college. However, physics students can also gain valuable experience by taking entry-level jobs or **internships** as research assistants or laboratory technicians. Students who pursue these kinds of positions often increase their chances of being accepted into graduate degree programs.

Education

A **bachelor's degree** is the first step to becoming a physicist. A student must then complete master's and **doctoral degrees** to be considered for most jobs in this field. Postgraduate study is required for many positions. For most people, this means attending college for a total of 8 to 10 years.

Application

Use the internet to learn where physicists work. Contact places that hire physicists. Talk to professors about research jobs. Apply for positions, and request job interviews.

Career Connections

Plan your physics career with this activity. Follow the instructions in the steps below to complete the process of becoming a physicist.

A Visit a physics lab at a university, hospital, or technology company. Talk to physicists. Ask them what they like about their work. Find out where they went to college.

B Decide if this is a job you want to do. Do you want to spend many hours doing research in a physics laboratory?

C Think about the skills you need to be a physicist. Physicists are interested in the way the world works. They are good at learning advanced math such as calculus. They do not mind spending months, and even years, on the same project.

D Visit an educational fair at a college that teaches physics classes. Find out which high school classes prepare you to pursue a physics degree.

1. Think about how you can get work experience while at college. Meet with your professors. Ask them about summer jobs. Volunteer for college research projects.

2. Attend career fairs at your college. Talk to people who hire physicists. Ask for advice on how to apply for a job. Find out where their companies post job information.

3. Follow physics job sites on the internet. Apply for jobs with companies and colleges. Look for jobs on university and research facility websites.

4. Be well prepared for a job interview. Research the organization. Know what it does. Make a list of questions about the job offered. Employers will ask questions about your education. Tell them about your work experience, too.

Quiz

1. What is physics?
2. Which U.S. state employs the most physicists?
3. What does an astrophysicist study?
4. What is the first step of the scientific method?
5. What is the purpose of a plotting compass?

6. Which form of electromagnetic radiation led to the discovery of DNA's structure?
7. In which country were balance scales first created?
8. At which school subject do many future physicists excel?
9. How many years of college does a physicist usually have to complete?
10. What percentage of university physics teachers in the United States are female?

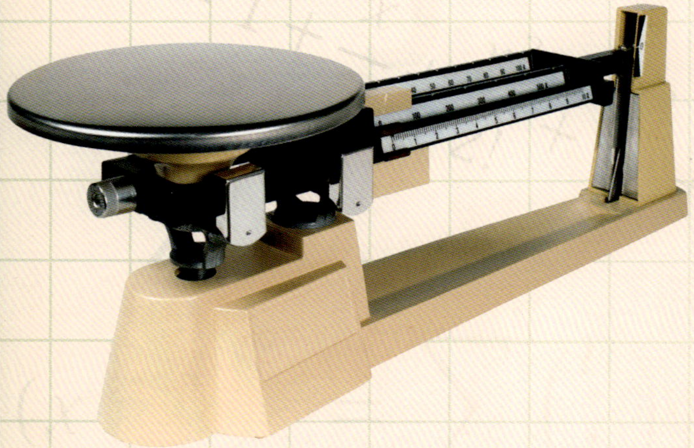

Answers

1. The science of matter and energy
2. California
3. Objects and events in space
4. Ask a question
5. To measure magnetic fields
6. X-ray
7. Egypt
8. Math
9. About 8 to 10
10. 21 percent

Key Words

algebra: a branch of mathematics that substitutes letters for numbers

bachelor's degree: the first level of a college program of study

black holes: places in space where gravity pulls so much that even light cannot get out

calculus: a branch of mathematics that involves the study of rates of change

density: a measurement that compares the amount of matter an object has to its volume

doctoral degrees: the highest level of college programs of study

electromagnetic radiation: energy with electric and magnetic field components

fossil fuels: energy sources, such as coal or gas, that formed in the ground long ago

gamma ray: high-energy electromagnetic radiation

genetic: relating to heredity, or the sharing of traits

internships: positions in which students learn how a specific job works

magnetic fields: areas under the influence of a magnetic charge

master's degrees: the second-highest level of college programs of study

matter: any type of material

mechanics: a branch of engineering dealing with motion and forces

renewable resources: materials that can be used repeatedly and replaced naturally

satellite: a machine that moves through space and sends information back to Earth

simulation: a model of a real-life or hypothetical situation

supernovas: stars that have exploded

theories: ideas that are intended to explain facts or events

vacuum chambers: enclosures from which nearly all matter has been removed

Index

Published by AV2
14 Penn Plaza 9th Floor
New York, NY 10122
Website: www.av2books.com

Library of Congress Cataloging-in-Publication Data

Names: Gagne, Tammy, author. | Kissock, Heather, author.
Title: Physicist / Tammy Gagne.
Other titles: STEM careers (AV2)
Description: New York : AV2, 2021. | Series: STEM careers |
Includes index. | Audience: Ages 9-12. | Audience: Grades 4-6.
Identifiers: LCCN 2019041019 (print) | LCCN 2019041020 (ebook) | ISBN 9781791116927 (library binding) |
ISBN 9781791116934 (paperback) | ISBN 9781791116941 | ISBN 9781791116958
Subjects: LCSH: Physics--Vocational guidance--Juvenile literature. | Physicists--Juvenile literature.
Classification: LCC QC29 .G34 2020 (print) | LCC QC29 (ebook) | DDC 530.023--dc23
LC record available at https://lccn.loc.gov/2019041019
LC ebook record available at https://lccn.loc.gov/2019041020

Printed in Guangzhou, China
1 2 3 4 5 6 7 8 9 0 24 23 22 21 20

052020
101119

Project Coordinator: Heather Kissock
Designer: Ana María Vidal

The publisher acknowledges Getty Images, Alamy, iStock, Shutterstock, and Wikimedia Commons as its primary image suppliers for this title.